BYE BYE BROADWAY

Telegraph & Argus

BYE BYE BROADWAY

A PICTORIAL HISTORY OF BRADFORD CITY CENTRE

breedon **books**
PUBLISHING

First published in Great Britain in 2005 by

The Breedon Books Publishing Company Limited

Breedon House, 3 The Parker Centre, Derby, DE21

4SZ.

ISBN 1 85983 489 2

Printed and bound by Cromwell Press, Trowbridge,
Wiltshire

Contents

Foreword

'Change is not made without inconvenience, even from worse to better'. So, according to Samuel Johnson in the Preface to his *English Dictionary*, said the great Anglican theologian, Richard Hooker.

Hooker was talking about his 'big idea' – the belief that the church should be a tolerant and inclusive body, broad enough to encompass many different forms of Christian belief in order that as many people as possible should worship God.

What he would have made of the multi-cultural, multi-ethnic, multi-faith nature of modern Bradford will never be known, but his fundamental belief in tolerance would have made a fitting backdrop to the efforts of the majority of its citizens today to forge a harmonious, peaceful, cohesive and humane society in the fourth largest metropolitan district in the country.

What Hooker recognised was that change – be it social or physical – does not come without disruption and, often, discomfort.

Bradford's wrestle with social change has been more than matched over many decades by its tussle with physical upheaval. As I write, the city centre is in the throes of another reincarnation as the 1960s-built Broadway precinct area – itself a controversial re-modelling of a Victorian hotch-potch which today would have been the subject of countless conservation orders – is torn down to make way for a £300 million shopping scheme.

The project is merely the latest chapter in the chequered history of this great city's heart, a message we have attempted to portray in the choice of material for this book. I am indebted to DAVID BARNETT for his work in organising and co-ordinating the content; to ALAN MAGSON for his painstaking research and cataloguing of the precious glass photographic plates which provided many of the images; and to JIM GREENHALF and MIKE PRIESTLEY for much of the text and many of the captions.

It is a fascinating story and one that will doubtless continue into the far-flung future. It will be generations before we know whether the efforts of our early 21st-century planners have stood the test of time.

It is certain, though, that we will suffer much 'inconvenience' in the meanwhile, some of which may be assuaged by reflecting through these pages on how others have suffered before us!

Perry Austin-Clarke
EDITOR
Telegraph & Argus

Chapter One

The Changing Face of Bradford

In 1835, the painter John Wilson Anderson stood on a grassy hill to the north-east of Bradford and painted what he saw in the valley below.

A dozen or more slender factory chimneys rise from the vicinity of the Bradford Beck, among them the tower of the parish church. In the foreground cows sit in a bosky meadow, perhaps anticipating rain in the clouds banking up over the western horizon.

The painting captures Bradford on the eve of its change from a rural trading settlement to a factory town. The railway was coming, steam-powered engines inside gigantic palaces of industry.

Within half a century the small hillside hamlets that Anderson had painted were lost in a forest of tall chimneys and church spires. The largely rural idyll of the start of the Industrial Revolution was becoming a manufacturing and trading powerhouse, which mined vast quantities of coal and iron ore, made machinery of all sorts, imported wool from Australia and the hair of llamas from Peru, and sold its goods all over the globe.

The record we have of this change is an unnamed engraving of Bradford from Cliff Quarry. The presence of the Town Hall's Tuscan tower dates the picture as post-1873. In the foreground, men labour at cutting and moving huge blocks of sandstone for future grand buildings. Not a field nor a cow can be seen.

In the 170 years between John Wilson Anderson's painting and the publication of this book Bradford has endured many ups and downs. For example: slumps in trade, two recessions, several riots and a cholera epidemic that killed hundreds. Changes in the make-up of its population reflected dire political and economic circumstances in Ireland and Central Europe in the 19th century and altered manufacturing conditions at home in the 20th century. Bradford absorbed thousands of Irish Catholics, German Jews, Italians, Poles, Pakistani Muslims, Sikhs, Hindus and Afro-Caribbeans, as well as people from other parts of Britain. Political oppression in Africa and the expansion of the European Union to 25 member states brought several thousand more people from Africa and Eastern Europe in the first few years of the 21st century. The diminution of engineering and mass textile manufacturing in Bradford has only been partly offset by chemicals, high-tech electronics, education, a large public sector in terms of local and central government and an expanding service sector.

Bradford made cloth, clothes, marine engines, cars, aeroplanes, tractors, televisions, modems for telephones, computers, set-top boxes and guidance systems for weapons of war. It produced entrepreneurs, manufacturers, social reformers, education, health and welfare pioneers, musicians, painters, writers, Olympic athletes, architects and visionary public officials.

From 1835 to 2005 Bradford changed from a village to a town to a city, and for a time was the wool capital of the world. In 2001 the entire village of Saltaire was declared a World Heritage Site. Former Methodist chapels have become wholesale centres and curry houses. Mosques have moved out of terraced houses into custom-built constructions, erected and paid for in instalments. Converted textile mills now contain modern apartments. Whatever else it has been, over the past 170 years Bradford has proved to be dynamic – susceptible to change. Post-industrial cities risk becoming moribund unless they are prepared to accept and embrace change.

This book is principally a photographic and illustrated chronicle of architectural change spanning the seven decades of the Victorian and Edwardian eras, the years of World War One and World War Two, and the five decades of the second Elizabethan era. It was prompted by two separate occurrences: the discovery of a large number of previously unpublished photographs of the city centre in the T&A archives, and the Broadway shopping development. The latter entailed the demolition of some of the 1960s buildings for which a good deal of the city's Victorian heritage was needlessly sacrificed from the mid-1950s through to the mid-1970s.

The story of Bradford's changing face since 1835 took place in specific phases. The first phase concerns those building controls adopted by the new town council in the late 1840s and early 1850s, which directed all of the important civic and architectural changes for the next quarter of a century. The second major phase was begun shortly after World War Two when a central development master plan was conceived and Stanley Wardley was brought in from Wakefield as Bradford Corporation's city engineer to drive it through. This phase lasted until the mid-1970s. A minor phase occurred in the mid-1980s, but this was unplanned office development, largely speculative building done on the back of a national boom fed by four billion pounds worth of tax cuts by Margaret Thatcher's Chancellor of the Exchequer Nigel Lawson. Bradford tried desperately to engineer significant developments in the 1990s, most of which, like the Odsal Superdome, the Lister City project, the West End development and the Forster Square Burton's shopping scheme, came to nothing. The present Forster Square retail park, Leisureland at Vicar Lane, the proliferation of drinking emporiums at the lower end of Great Horton Road and the electrification of the Aire Valley railway represent the epoch's successes. The four or five years of the 21st century saw the beginning of what many hope will turn out to be another major phase of Bradford's evolution.

According to an article by Geoffrey Manuel in *The Bradford Antiquary* of 1991, in 1850 the recently incorporated borough council of Bradford obtained a local Act of Parliament, the Bradford Improvement Act, which brought together clauses from the Public Health Act and two others and repealed provisions of earlier acts.

'The powers of these various Acts of Parliament were ceded to bring some order to the chaotic and uncontrolled growth of Bradford which, in common with other nineteenth century industrial towns, was struggling with the social and health problems of rapid urbanisation,' Geoffrey Manuel says. In other words, Bradford's local authority needed to be empowered if it was to assist in the delivery of economic regeneration.

The year 1850 marks the beginning of local authority planning control, which required proper building plans to be deposited with officials at the Town Hall. Plans included a separate note of the type of property being proposed, a reference to its location, name of owner and architect and details of the drains, an important public health requirement. The plans were studied and signed off as approved or disapproved. If accepted the plans were serially numbered in sequence. Plan No.1, dated 15 October 1850, submitted by local architects Andrews and Delauney, was for 17 houses in Lumb Lane for the Crown Building Society. It was approved within three days! The final plan in the series, No.100299, dated 30 January 1974, was for a garage at Wibsey. After April 1974 local government was handed over to the Bradford Metropolitan District Council.

Geoffrey Manuel's invaluable research shows the scale and the speed with which booming Bradford bounded forwards. In 1852/53, for example, the corporation's Building & Improvement Committee dealt with plans for 71 new streets and 1,772 new buildings, including 48 warehouses and mills. The following year produced plans for 68 new streets and 1,669 new buildings. Virtually the entire area that we know as Little Germany was developed in the 20 years from 1853. At this point in the story of Bradford's changing face mention needs to be made of the architects who designed the best of the city and its surrounding environs that we value today.

The most famous were Henry Lockwood and William Mawson, who came here from Hull in the 1840s and won commissions for Salts Mill and the village of Saltaire, St George's Hall, the Wool Exchange, the Town Hall (now City Hall), the Victoria Hotel and St Luke's Hospital.

William Andrews and Joseph Pepper designed the Theatre Royal in Manningham Lane and the Mechanics' Institute, which was located in a triangular block between Aldermanbury and the Town Hall. Both the theatre and the institute were demolished, but other examples of their work are Manningham Mills, Church House, North Parade and Bradford Commercial bank in Hustlergate.

Eli Milnes and Charles France designed many of the mercantile warehouses and offices in Little Germany (Andrews and Delauney designed others), as well as Thornton Baths and wash-houses, Swan Arcade (demolished) and an extension to Bradford Royal Infirmary.

James Ledingham designed the Yorkshire Penny Bank, St Catherine's House in Manningham and houses on the Rosse estate, Heaton.

There were others. Their work was commented upon. In their day the architects of Victorian Bradford were notable public figures. Many of their modern counterparts do not enjoy either the same sort of acclaim or public respect. The explanation for this is simple: the abominations of the 1960s and 1970s imposed on Bradford by a local authority master plan, which were opposed in vain by many Bradfordians. Ironically, many of the buildings representing the proposed brave new world of Queen Elizabeth II's post-war 20th century Bradford are scheduled for the bulldozer and the wrecking ball. What was intended by Stanley Wardley to be a modern aristocracy of buildings is heading for the chop. How cheap and tawdry those designs seem to us – the through-city road system drastically altering the sight lines of how

Bradford had evolved – yet in the early 1950s they must have looked impressive on paper and in model form.

The new Bradford, geared principally for the convenience of motor vehicles, was going to be seen as the old one rarely was. Local authority bye-laws were enacted which enforced a drastic clean-up of the atmosphere. Like unwanted phantoms, the acrid fogs and smogs which had been the burgeoning city's legacy since the proliferation of factories and mills from 1835 onwards were banished. Many of our photographs reveal the fall out of grime and dirt on most of central Bradford's buildings. Even on clear days the city looked as though it was permanently in mourning. Bradford's Clean Air Acts remain among the greatest of the benefits bequeathed by local politicians to posterity. The changing face of Bradford was unveiled and many were amazed by what they saw. This pocket industrial Hercules of the Aire Valley had a marvellous panorama of surrounding moorland, farmland and countryside. And on clear days skies to rival those of Montana and South Dakota. At night, from the heights of Wrose, Bingley, Baildon and Queensbury, Bradford resembled nothing so much as the vast bivouacked encampment of a Napoleonic army, the darkness illuminated by swirling patterns of twinkling, flickering lights.

But just as beauty was revealed, so too was ugliness exposed. In February 1962 the poet and architectual aesthete John Betjeman delivered his verdict. He described Stanley Wardley's modern Bradford as 'international nothingness'. With the odd modification, that is how the city remained for the best part of the next 40 years. Among the modifications were some fine modern public sculptures to complement the plethora of 19th-century statuary. Ian Judd's statue of J.B. Priestley, Ian Randall's *Fibres* at St Blaise Square leading into the repositioned Forster Square railway station, flanked by that array of wonderful arches, and Timothy Shutter's *Grandad's Clock and Chair* sculpture in Little Germany, are three examples. The Brian Lynch Memorial Garden at Hall Ings, the Theatre in the Mill on the University of Bradford campus and, at Lister Park, the Boat House and the Moghul Garden are also quality additions to Bradford's amenities. Centenary Square is perhaps a little too utilitarian and spartan.

As for the rest, the three 10-year master plans proposed for Airedale, Manningham and Central Bradford, we can only surmise and hope for the best. Only one thing is certain, the face of Bradford will continue to change.

Broadway – now the subject of so much busy work and planning – as it was in 1972.

An aerial view of the city centre taken in 1977.

Across the rooftops of central Bradford in 1972.

View from Westgate showing the rooftop car park of the Kirkgate Centre in 1982.

Forster Square, now under massive redevelopment, photographed in 1973.

Buses at Bradford Interchange in 1977.

The Alhambra and
the Odeon – still
open and showing
movies in 1989.

A wonderful view across
Bradford from the City
Hall clock tower in 1996.

The domes and spires of Bradford, 1982.

The City Hall clock marks the passage of time… but what will the future hold for Bradford?

Chapter Two

From the Victorians to the Forties

The first half of the 20th century saw Bradford grow from the collection of mills and associated housing seen in landscape paintings of the district from a century before into a powerhouse of industry and culture. In 1904 an industrial exhibition was held in Bradford, the same year that the Cartwright Memorial Hall was built. The Alhambra Theatre opened in 1914.

The first council houses in Bradford were built in 1907, while in 1919 the church of St Peter was made Bradford Cathedral. Bradford Royal Infirmary was built in 1936.

The Jowett company began making cars in 1910 and did so until 1954. The twenties and thirties saw the beginning of the decline of the textile industry, although new industries came in.

And despite the best efforts of the Luftwaffe, Bradford survived the bombing runs and emerged largely unscathed in architectural terms.

This was the view in the first half of the 20th century from the gods in the Mechanics Institute, later demolished and now the site of Centenary Square.

Passers-by look on at a partly-covered cable trench in Kirkgate in 1904, a sign of increasing progress. Nowadays, of course, Bradford is no stranger to roadworks…

Horse-drawn carriages on Market Street, probably in the 1890s. Note the second driver along, having a rest before his next journey.

An 1883 artist's impression of Kirkgate, with famous Bradford jewellers and goldsmiths Fattorini's on the corner.

A postcard image to mark the opening of the Mechanics Institute in 1871.

This 1880 ink drawing shows the long-gone Swan Arcade in all its splendour, shortly after it was constructed and opened.

The statue of Sir Titus Salt used to sit opposite City Hall. Now it reposes in Lister Park.

A stylised graphic of the interior of Kirkgate Market. The date is unknown, but it looks to be around the turn of the 20th century.

The dark, Satanic mills of Bradford are really in evidence here, in this view of the city from Cliff Quarry.

Bradford in 1835, as painted by John Wilson Anderson. The chimneys are in evidence but it is a hugely pared-down vision of the community we know today. Bradford, of course, wasn't a city until 1897.

The diamond jubilee of Queen Victoria was a cause for celebration across the country, and this drawing of City Hall in 1897 shows the building dressed for the occasion.

A T&A reader found an old milk jug bearing this drawing of Bradford's City Hall. There was speculation that it was made to commemorate the building – then the Town Hall – being opened in 1873.

A huge procession was held to mark the opening of Bradford Town Hall in 1873. Note from the umbrellas in the crowds that it wasn't a good day for a parade!

The bell for City Hall was hauled into place in August 1873, and crowds gathered to watch. The bell was named 'Matthew Williams', after the Lord Mayor in that year.

Hundreds gather for the laying of the foundation stone for Bradford Town Hall in 1870, with Sir Matthew Thompson, the then mayor, doing the honours.

An early 20th-century view of Bradford city centre.

This is the Anglo-South American Bank on Market Street, pictured in 1920. The bank was formed in 1889 as the Bank of Tarapaca and London, to foster trade between the UK and Chile. Now the building is occupied by the Old Bank pub.

Nowadays this is the Goose pub, but this picture, exact date unknown, shows it as Ann Teeke's jewellery, furniture and glass shop, with James Walsh tobacconists next door.

A view across the jumble of mid-20th-century rooftops, with Market Street running up the right-hand side of the picture. The superstructure imposed on the Brown, Muff & Co. building (centre) has since been removed.

The trolley-buses are out in force in this photograph of Bradford Town Hall Square in 1923.

Dating from 1938, this photograph shows the turntable at the Bradford Forster Square terminus.

Britannia House all lit up in 1938, as the trolley-bus cables criss-cross the street in front.

A nice aerial shot of
Bradford from the early
1950s, with the Exchange
Station central in the
picture.

Forster Square in 1936, photographed from what was then the General Post Office.

The junction of Hall Ings and Leeds Road being gradually demolished in connection with Bradford's Central Area plan in 1938.

Looking across from Foster Square at a huge swathe of land being redeveloped.

The New Victoria theatre in the early thirties, now the derelict Odeon Building. Notice the show 'Follies of 1980' advertised above the entrance; this was an error and should have read 'Follies of 1890'.

The New Victoria Ballroom, part of the entertainment complex that is now the old Odeon cinema site. It opened in 1930 and this glittering venue remained open until 1964.

The new Victoria Cinema, later the Gaumont and then the Odeon.

The interior of the Gaumont cinema.

The foyer before the crowds rushed into the New Victoria, which opened in 1930.

The New Victoria theatre and cinema on opening day in 1930.

A rooftop view from City Hall towards Kirkgate Market, in 1948.

Dating from 1948, this was actually a New Year greetings card showing the Alhambra, which was sent out by the Lord Mayor to Bradford soldiers still serving in Japan after World War Two.

The rabbit warren of streets
stretching from the corner of
Thornton Road up Godwin Street
in 1948.

The Alhambra in
1949, with one Lilac
Domino top of the bill
for the coming
attractions.

Bradfordians inspect bomb damage in Brunswick Place in 1941.

Workmen paint kerbstones in August 1939 so that Bradfordians could see the edge of roads during the inevitable blackouts to come.

The back entrance of Lingard's store, which was damaged after a bombing raid by the Lufwaffe at the end of August 1940.

December 1948. A high-level shot along Broadway, showing open land on the corner of Charles Street, later the C&A store.

Peel Place at the
bottom of Leeds
Road, with its statue
of Sir Robert Peel,
July 1949.

PEEL

The New Inn pub in Victoria Square, with roadworks taking place outside a little before Christmas 1948.

A busy shopping scene showing Kirkgate at its junction with Darley Street in 1948.

Bradford city centre under water during the devastating floods of 1947.

Chapter Three

The Fifties

After the war, the decline of the textile industry continued but Bradford's economy as a whole began to boom, and more and more industries sprang up in the city, from tractor manufacture to companies making televisions.

More and more people found themselves in clerical work – banking, insurance, civil service and local government became major employers.

The fifties was also notable for a massive change in Bradford that was more demographic than topographic – it was the decade that saw the biggest influx of immigrants into the city.

More and more council housing was built and major redevelopment occurred in the city centre, with the advent of what became known as the Wardley plan.

The first trolleybus in Broadway, June 1954.

Excavating building foundations on Broadway, March 1959.

April 1957: demolition of buildings in Bridge Street.

The top of
Broadway near what
was the Ritz cinema.
The decorations are
for the 1953
Coronation of
Queen Elizabeth II.

February 1958: a
hole in Broadway
that was to become
C&A.

May 1950: looking down Broadway towards Forster Square.

A rainy July day in 1956. A view of Broadway showing the Ritz on the right and the Swan Arcade at middle left.

Window-shopping in the elegant Swan Arcade.

The Swan Arcade interior.

December 1958. It is noon in Swan Arcade.

More of the same.

December 1959: Swan Arcade without festive decorations.

November 1957: like much of central Bradford, Swan Arcade was grim with industrial pollution on the outside but clean and business-like on the inside.

An undated exterior photograph of Swan Arcade in the 1950s.

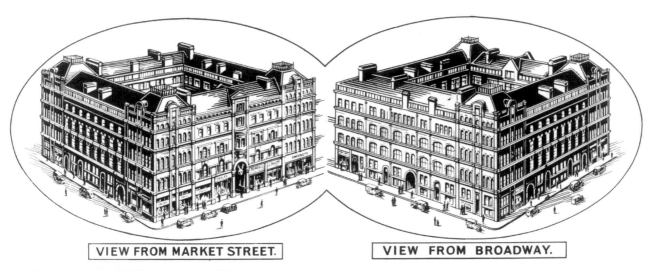

Two drawings of different views of Swan Arcade.

March 1962: Swan Arcade's entrance is shut, the scaffolding is up and the building is about to come down.

The Swan Arcade before demolition in 1962, from Market Street.

August 1962: a crowd watches the dying Swan, the destruction of a great building. Across Market Street are the Wool Exchange and Brown Muffs with all the roof structure (since removed).

Forster Square in the 1950s, seen through a web of trolleybus wires. A policeman directs road vehicles rather than traffic lights.

Spring 1952. No fewer than four corporation gardeners tend the grass and flowers around the statue of Edward Forster in the public place named after him.

The Post Office building fronting the Cathedral in Forster Square.

December 1952: note the public seating has been removed from around the central triangle of Forster Square. Forster Square station, as it was, is at the top.

December 1958: new model Bradford, from City Hall in the foreground to the Cathedral at the top of the picture.

June 1950: unrecognisable today, Forster Square as it was, seen from the Cathedral side.

People enjoying the sunshine and flowers in Forster Square.

May 1950: The old YMCA Forster Square/Canal Road junction, and not a man in a hard hat in sight.

May 1957: the view across Valley Parade at the end of the football season. In the background is the old Midland Road power station.

Years before Centenary Square was created, there was plenty of on-street car parking at City Hall.

John Street Market (now the Oastler Centre) as it was nearly 50 years ago.

The same, undergoing improvements.

March 1958: on the left is Market Street leading down into Petergate. On the right the Ritz Cinema leads down to Broadway.

NOTICE

VEHICLES OF ANY KIN
ARE NOT ALLOWED TO PASS
ALONG OR STOP IN THE
MARKET AVENUES FOR AN
PURPOSE BETWEEN THE HOURS
OF ... ...
& 8.30 a.m. SATURDAYS 10...
BY ORDER.

John Street Market and street
stalls selling flowers.

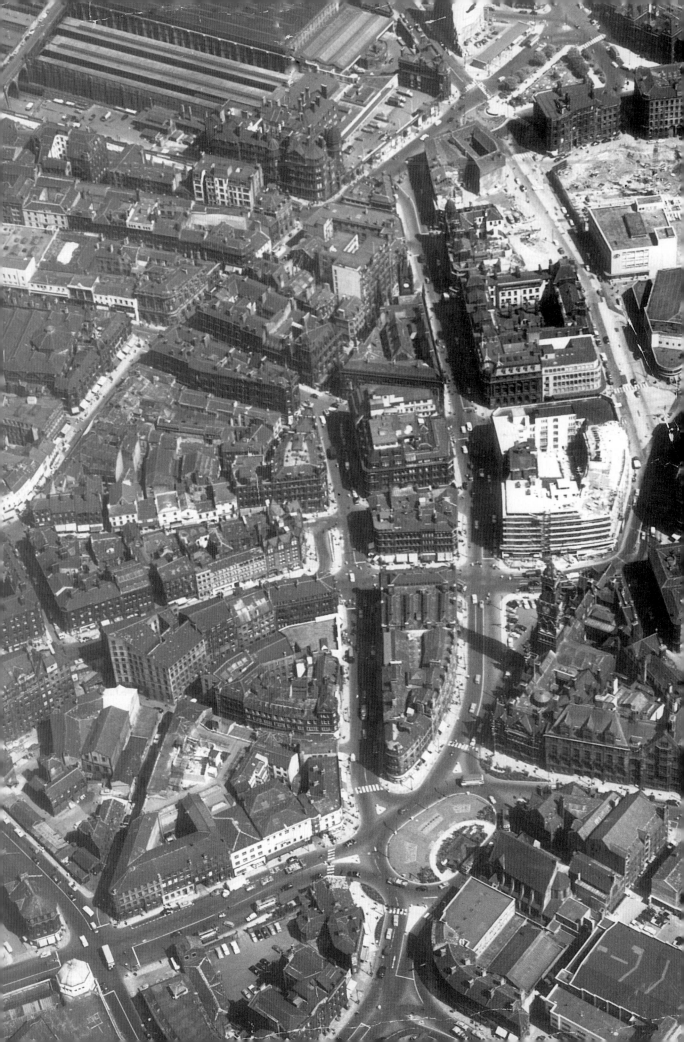

(Opposite page) Thornton Road traffic island, lower centre. All the buildings in the bottom right were demolished to make way for the police HQ and magistrates courts.

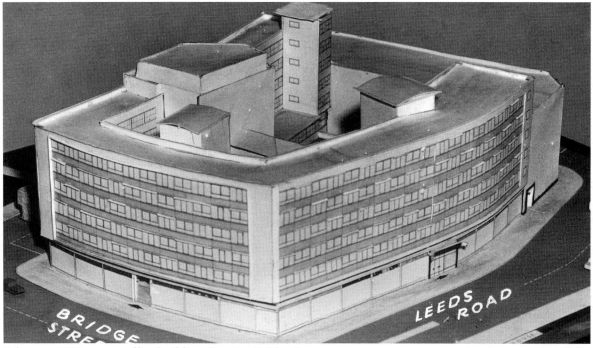

February 1958: a new office building fronting Bridge Street.

November 1959: this corporation model shows Exchange Station on the mid-left and on the mid-right what used to be a goods depot.

January 1959: the same model from another angle, this time being studied (for the camera) by two wool-suited gentlemen.

August 1959: top right is the Victoria Hotel. Directly left is Exchange Station. Swan Arcade and the Wool Exchange face one another across Market Street at lower right. The central demolition area goes from Broadway to Hall Ings.

July 1958: across from City Hall tower that triangular chunk of buildings was flattened to make way for the National & Provincial buildings, which were demolished in September 2002.

From City Hall in the foreground to St George's Hall mid-right and the T&A. The other buildings in Drake Street were demolished.

Westwards out of the city centre with Westgate leading into White Abbey Road at the top and Thornton Road at the bottom.

Note the startling absence of traffic on Hall Ings, left of centre, and what is becoming Broadway, in the centre.

A marvellous view of Town Hall Square
with Thornton Road directly opposite.
The glass-roofed toilets on the left of the
traffic island were a landmark.

City Hall and what used to be the traffic island where Thornton Road came right into the city centre.

A policeman on point duty in front of Forster Square.

A gloomy day in late November 1955, with the arched roofs of Exchange Station in the background.

This view is believed to be of Hall Ings going into Leeds Road and was subsequently demolished. The other Bentley Street is in Wyke.

Lingard's clothing store on the corner of Market Street and Forster Square.

An old watering hole in Market Street, no longer in existence.

May 1953: a building at Westgate decorated for the Coronation.

Bridge House going up in the city centre.

Cobbled Sunbridge Road, leading up to Sunwin House.

The buildings in the foreground made way for the 'banana' block of new buildings in Petergate.

April 1957: the site of what is now the Goose café-bar. The building left standing is now the Old Bank pub.

August 1959. Most people seem to have walked, judging by this scene, thought to be in Leeds Road.

October 1957. The Charles Street/Hall Ings junction.

The statue of Sir Robert Peel comes down in 1957 for the road-widening scheme.

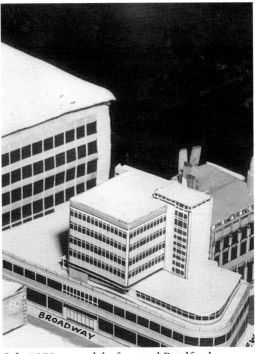

July 1958: a model of central Bradford.

November 1958: more old buildings about to bite the dust.

Two pictures showing celebrations marking the visit of Queen Elizabeth II to Bradford on 28 October 1954.

September 1950: traffic policemen used to be common. With modern road developments they were replaced by masses of traffic lights. But at 10.40am in the morning there's no traffic about.

5 June 1953: Victoria Square. The roundabout has gone. Buildings on both sides of the picture were demolished for the police HQ and Prince's Way.

September 1950: a photograph taken the same day from another side of City Hall, looking towards the New Vic Cinema and the Alhambra.

September 1950: City Hall is on the right, with the old Provincial Building Society opposite, now demolished. Note the tram too.

Chapter Four

The Sixties

The 1960s saw perhaps the most radical changes in Bradford's topography, with what became known as the Wardley era.

Although Stanley Wardley's plans for the redevelopment of Bradford city centre were first unveiled in 1953, it was after his death in 1965 that the majority of his visions were realised.

The Bradford Corporation's chief engineer drew up a plan which included the wholesale destruction of acres of Victorian warehousing and offices, and which saw the character of Forster Square, Bridge Street up to the junction with Thornton Road, the bottom of Manchester Road, the Nelson Street area and Drake Street, all changed utterly.

The demolition of the Victorian Swan Arcade perhaps drew most brickbats for the scheme, which also saw the opening of the Magistrate's Court, the Interchange and the Arndale Centre, now the Kirkgate shopping mall.

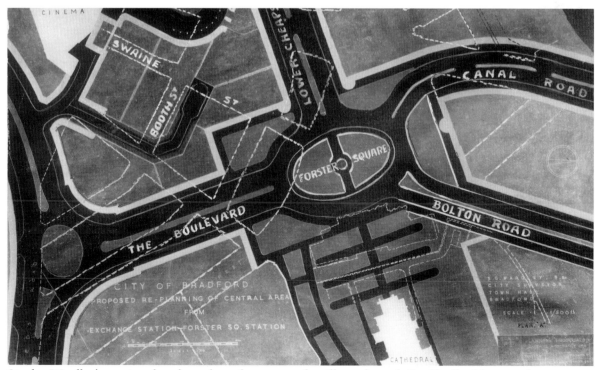

Stanley Wardley's master plan shows how the new roads will cut through Bradford's old street plan.

Many Bradfordians wish the Cathedral did look like this – without the old Post Office building blocking the view.

Again, the master plan imposed on historic Bradford.

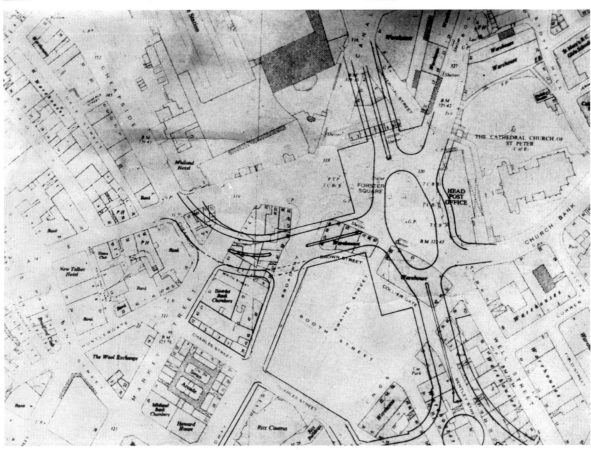

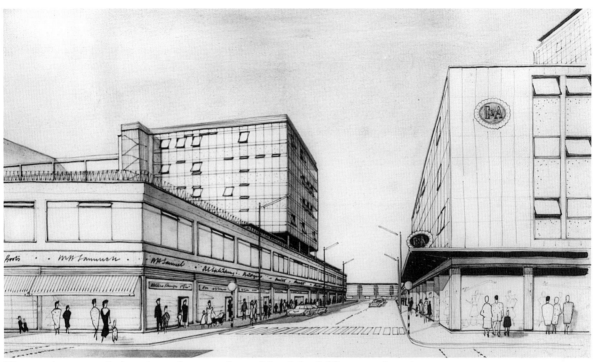

How to destroy a city's unique character by making it look like any other city centre.

(Right) June 1966: Union Street was renamed Hall Ings. An uninspiring hotel was built. The civic gardens were uprooted in the mid-1990s to make way for the Brian Lynch Memorial Garden.

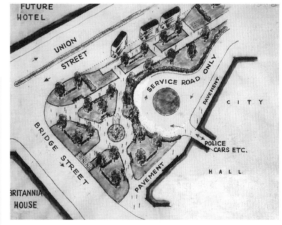

Some of Bradford's 1960s buildings scheduled for the bulldozer.

The drawing makes the Petergate building look imposing. Within a few years its Portland stone cladding looked dirty and weather-worn.

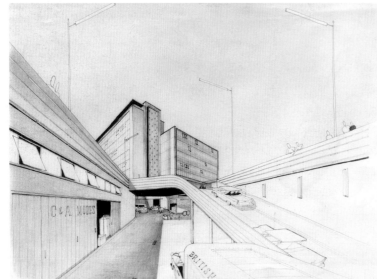

(Above) Planning a thoroughly characterless modern look.

The back way up to the car park between British Home Stores, WH Smith and other Broadway shops.

(Below) Broadway as it was to become.

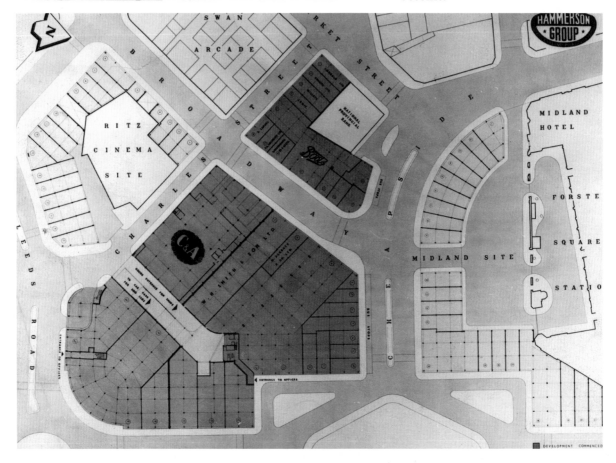

(*Above*) February 1963: in the midst of the coldest winter since 1947. The new Bradford is visible above Forster Square.

September 1964. Motorists are advised to stay three car lengths behind one another at 30mph.

(*Below*) October 1963: the erection of the NCP car park across from City Hall.

February 1967: a queue of traffic coming down Church Bank waits to negotiate the new Forster Square.

July 1962. City Hall, more than 43 years ago.

July 1963: either side of the T&A and Victoria Hotel in this panoramic picture so many buildings were to disappear.

September 1962. The interior of the old Forster Square station.

June 1964: the ornate gates of Forster Square station.

August 1966, when parcels used to go by rail from Forster Square.

July 1968: the goods yard at City Road, which no longer exists.

March 1963: as the station used to be before it was moved a quarter of a mile out of the city centre in the 1990s.

April 1964. Bridge Street at the junction with Union Street (Hall Ings).

(*Below and right*) Two photographs taken from City Hall with the twin domes of the Gaumont cinema (later the Odeon) and Morley Street to the left of the Alhambra.

Jacob's Well roundabout and subway under construction.

Smoky Bradford before the Corporation's clean air bye-laws were enacted in the late 1950s.

(Right and next page) December 1965: some things old and some things new in the very centre of Bradford.

August 1967: on the left, the old Victoria Square; in the centre, the block of buildings bulldozed to make way for the police HQ and the magistrates court.

TRAFFIC ISLAND

August 1962: re-aligning the roads from Petergate into Forster Square.

From the direction of Bradford Cathedral looking down into Cheapside.

The corner of Charles Street and Broadway, un-pedestrianised, in August 1962.

July 1964: civic dignitaries are shown Bradford's modern shops and offices. Central House is to the right.

December 1964: looking across from Little Germany at one of the 'improvements' on the corner of Hall Ings.

Nineteenth-century warehousing is removed to make way for an expanded Forster Square.

May 1960: the building of Broadway looking towards Bank Street.

December 1960: Christmas was a week away when this photograph of a rooftop car park near Broadway was taken.

The star-filled Shirley MacClaine movie, *What a Way to Go*, gives away the date of this photograph – 1963. This Art Deco Odeon, in Manchester Road, was demolished.

June 1963: demolition of a
multi-storey building in
the vicinity of the old
Exchange Station.

In 1969, the year of this photograph, the Gaumont, near the Alhambra theatre, became Bradford's only remaining Odeon cinema.

The imposing facade of Kirkgate Market. Note the double step near the roadway.

October 1962: cherry trees and grassy hillocks replaced these old buildings near City Hall.

April 1968: lorries carrying sacks of wool were a common sight in Bradford 40 years ago.

This photograph was taken from the St George's Hall side of Hall Ings.

The Wool Exchange becomes visible as the Swan Arcade is torn down.

The new Library Theatre taking shape. Eventually the theatre made way for the Pictureville Cinema.

The National & Provincial HQ going up opposite City Hall. It was demolished in September 2002.

Mourners or merely curious citizens look at the scar on the landscape that was Swan Arcade.

A photograph taken in the vicinity of Westgate.

June 1961: the junction of Godwin Street and Sunbridge Road.

Chapter Five

The Seventies

Local government re-organisation in 1974 saw Bradford become a Metropolitan District Council, but it wasn't just in City Hall that changes were being made.

Shopping in Bradford was being given an overhaul – the Kirkgate Centre opened in 1971 and six years later the Interchange transport hub was built to ease travel to and from the city centre for shoppers and commuters.

The Bradford we know now had pretty much taken shape by the end of the Seventies, with most of the large-scale redevelopment put forward under the auspices of Stanley Wardley being completed.

At the turn of the seventies, this picture from summer 1971 shows the old ABC cinema on Broadway.

Shoppers and office-workers take a break during the July heat of 1972 on Broadway.

Broadway in 1974.

Building work on Broadway as a large block of stone is craned into place.

Broadway has long been a place to meet up with others, relax while shopping or just watch the world go by, as this 1971 picture shows.

A 1972 view back towards the city centre, showing the cinema on the left, just hidden by a tree.

The Christmas decorations are still in place in mid-January 1972, but the wintry weather evidently doesn't hold much joy for these Broadway shoppers.

It might have been August, but that was no reason to take off your coat, at least according to these shoppers in 1972.

The X63 bound for Ilkley waits for a driver at the old Chester Street bus station, which used to be between the ice rink and the student's union building, October 1970.

Another shot of the Chester Street bus station's rain-soaked aprons, again from autumn 1970.

The Mechanics Institute was celebrating its centenary in 1971. It has since been demolished.

With what is now the In Plaice chip shop on the right of this photograph, and the clocktower of City Hall rising in the background, this picture shows the demolition-in-progress of the Mechanics Institute on what is now the edge of Centenary Square.

A busy shopping scene with the Mechanics Institute sandwiched between the window displays of shoe store Saxone, dating from 1972.

A locomotive rumbles onto the platform at the imposing old Exchange Station, a feat of Victorian engineering, in February 1972.

A view along the tracks into the massive Exchange Station in 1972. Within a few years it would be demolished.

Derelict and in the process of being razed, the once-proud Exchange Station is a shadow of its former self in 1976.

Cars parked alongside the Exchange Station in 1973. The site is now occupied by Bradford Crown Court.

A rather haunting photograph of a deserted Exchange Station in 1972.

The new replaces the old as work gets underway on building the Interchange railway station, while the hulking arches of the Exchange Station rust in the background in 1973.

Bradford city centre airport? No, a quirky accident of photography... a double exposure of Manchester Airport and the Exchange Station in Bradford in 1972.

The last train has now left the Exchange Station... demolition work begins in 1976.

Farewell to the age of steam as the demolition hammer brings down the old Exchange Station in 1976.

A quiet day outside John Street market.

In 1977 a fire damaged much of John Street market, but traders like this one carried on regardless by setting up shop in the street outside.

Fruit and veg on display at John Street market in 1970.

A family outing to John Street market in 1972.

Two of the Keystone Heads, which once adorned the entrance to Kirkgate Market, lie in the rubble as demolition gets underway in December 1973.

Feelings ran high when it was announced that the Kirkgate Market was to be demolished in 1973. Here, protesters pack a meeting.

Make-up, costumes and fake coffins were the order of the day when a march took place to protest about Kirkgate Market's closure.

Police officers have a word with one of the Kirkgate Market protesters.

The Godwin Street entrance to what was left of the Kirkgate Market in 1974, with the new market rising in the background.

The clowns might have been out in force but it was no laughing matter for this protester.

Rallying the crowds at the Kirkgate Market demolition protest in 1973.

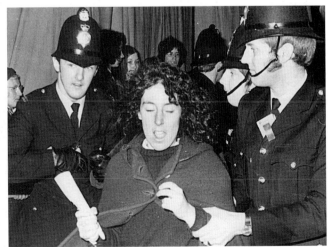

A protester is taken away after the Kirkgate Market closure protest.

Baxandall's café in Kirkgate Market, in 1972. Here you could get steak pie and peas for 11p and sausage roll and peas for the princely sum of 7p.

It was time for Kirkgate Market to finally face the music in this photograph from November 1973, with the demolition all but complete.

In 1972 Kirkgate Market was a thriving shopping area, as this picture shows.

The bulldozers move in on the Kirkgate Market site in 1973.

Diversions for traffic and pedestrians as Kirkgate Market is demolished.

The entrance to
Kirkgate Market
opening on to a
scene of
demolition in
1973.

BRADFORD MARKETS

The view from inside
Kirkgate Market as
demolition continues
apace in 1973.

The ornate frontage of Kirkgate Market as demolition takes place in 1973.

An impressive view of the old Bradford Power Station, which used to be on Canal Road, from 1977.

Smog from the Bradford Power Station on Canal Road adds to the 'dark Satanic mills' atmosphere of Bradford's skyline in 1970.

A controlled explosion brings one of the chimneys from the huge Bradford Power Station down as the site is demolished in 1979.

One of the cooling towers crumples dramatically as the Bradford Power Station on Canal Road is demolished.

With the imposing towers out of the way, work on clearing the Bradford Power Station site on Canal Road can continue, as shown in this picture from 1978.

In 1976 the now-busy Canal Road industrial estate was nothing more than cleared land.

The antics of this chap made front page news in the T&A on 24 July 1973. He was spotted clinging to the roof of City Hall and council worker Brian Appleyard is pictured trying to coax him down.

Firemen try to talk the man on top of City Hall off his perch.

Onlookers gather to watch the drama play out atop City Hall.

Police and firemen hold a tarpaulin sheet at ground level in case the worst happens.

A rooftop view of City Hall in 1975.

A fascinating view of the roofs across Bradford in 1972.

Looking across Hall Ings to what is now the NCP car park, from the vantage point of City Hall. Notice the vast area behind which is now the Interchange. This photograph dates from August 1972.

A rooftop view of
Provincial House in
1972, now demolished.

In 1971, this was the view from the multi-storey car park in Hall Ings, looking towards City Hall. The building site in the foreground is now the Hilton hotel.

On the site of the former Mechanics Institute, which is now Centenary Square, workers in 1974 lay out turf to create an open space which was quickly dubbed Bradford's own 'grassy knoll'.

In 1974, Queen Victoria looks across Bradford from her berth on City Hall.

An intriguing behind-the-scenes shot of maintenance taking place on the City Hall clock in 1972.

The police station is in the foreground of this picture, taken in 1974 from across the road in the National Museum of Photography, Film and Television.

An impressive bird's-eye view from City Hall in August 1972.

The view from the top of Provincial House, showing the inner ring road with the then new Central Library and Wardley House in the centre, in March 1970.

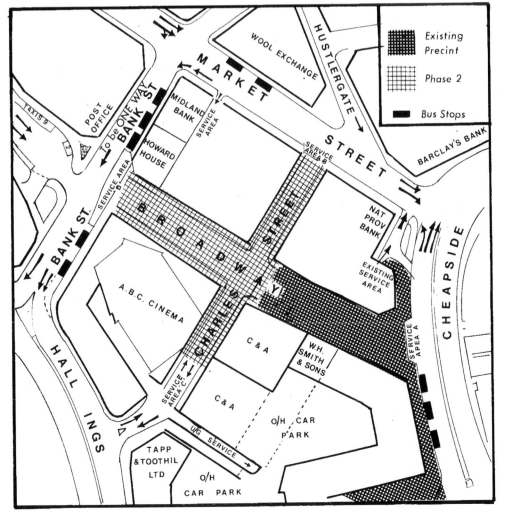

The Barclays Bank signage is prominent in the centre of this 1972 picture – it's now the Old Bank pub.

From 1971, this graphic shows the planned new shopping area for Broadway.

Taken on 5 November 1971, this picture of a smoggy Bradford city centre has plenty of smoke, although it is probably from the chimneys dotted around the city rather than Bonfire Night celebrations.

Chapter Six

The Eighties and Nineties

Development was slower in the eighties but the nineties saw a sea-change in the way people thought about Bradford.

Towards the end of the millennium, many people started to think about the city centre as a place in which to live as well as a place in which to work, shop and socialise.

By the late nineties the first planning applications were being prepared to take the old buildings which had fallen into disuse – especially the mills which had fallen silent with the decline of the textiles industry – and give them a new lease of life.

By the turn of the century, it became the norm to see old mills transformed into apartments and office blocks, and the positive way that people took to city centre living helped pave the way for the next stage in the redevelopment of Bradford – the Will Alsop master plan.

A rooftop view of central Bradford, looking from Westgate, in March 1985.

Looking down on Westgate and across the city in 1982. In the bottom right-hand corner you can just make out the Boy and Barrel pub.

The cars line up in the rooftop car park above the Kirkgate Centre in the centre of this picture from 1982.

John Street market, now the Oastler Centre, is at the right of this rooftop view from 1982.

Another rooftop scene showing the flats between Westgate and Grattan Road on the right.

The chapel which became the Bombay Brasserie and then the Koh-I-Noor restaurant can be seen on the right, with Lumb Lane heading off past the Drummond Mill chimney and towards Lister's Mill in the distance.

An excellent aerial view of Bradford looking north to Shipley, with the moors far beyond, from 1987.

An extremely evocative shot of Bradford at sundown, taken in 1980.

A map-like aerial plan
view of Bradford,
taken by the council in
1989.

Looking over the rooftops of Forster Square, into Cheapside, in 1986.

Bradford Cathedral forms the centrepiece for this impressive bird's eye view of Bradford around Forster Square and Little Germany in November 1987.

A cold January day from the air… Provincial House is just off-centre and the domes of the Odeon are a little further to the right. This picture was taken in 1989.

Bradford's industrial heritage is well to the fore in this atmospheric shot from 1982.

The Alhambra is in the foreground and the sheer size of the Odeon buildings just above it can be gauged from this aerial shot from 1989.

The Forster Square offices in 1986, now demolished to make way for the new Broadway redevelopment.

City Hall is resplendent in the centre of this aerial shot from January 1989.

The Christmas lights over Broadway in 1984.

Christmas at Broadway in the 1990s.

August 1985, with C&A in focus on Broadway.

Forster Square Station forecourt found a new use in the mid-1980s as a venue for car-boot sales.

It's the morning rush-hour in October 1987 and commuters stream from the latest arrival at Forster Square station.

The Midland Hotel towers over the station forecourt and its parked cars with the railway frontage wall still intact in 1989.

The winter rush for summer holidays is on as the queues form at Sunwin House's travel desk in November 1985.

Flyposting was a menace in the early 1990s, giving a new style of decor to the closed-down Howdens Sewing Shop at the junction of James Street and John Street.

Sunwin House in all its
Art Deco glory, with the
now-replaced office
block on the far corner
of Godwin Street on
the left, in 1985.

The Alhambra dome, supported only by steel girders, during the controversial £8.5 million facelift in the mid-1980s, which turned it into one of the country's top theatres.

A 1999 aerial shot of the city centre, with the new bars yet to be built in the leafy triangle in the foreground between Morley Street and Great Horton Road, where Glyde House still stood in splendid isolation.

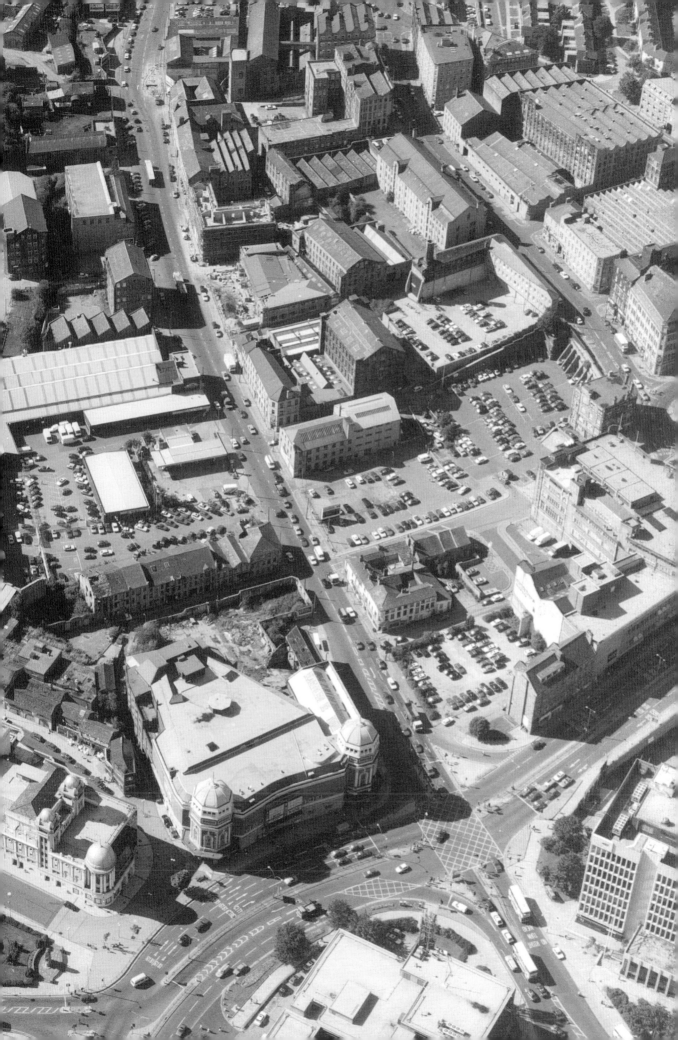

The road to nowhere….The yet-to-be-opened M606, pictured in August 1972, appears to vanish into a tunnel beneath the roundabout at Rooley Lane, awaiting an extension towards the city centre that was never constructed.

Traffic passing in front of City Hall in the mid-1990s before the road was closed and Centenary Square was created.

Many of these floral trees had to go when the city's 'seaside theme' square was created in Norfolk Gardens behind City Hall.

A carved mouse, the signature of Yorkshire furniture-maker 'Mousey' Thompson, on one of the legs of the Lord Mayor's chair in City Hall.

The frame of the building set to be home to the Inland Revenue starts to take shape in 1996 on the site of the former Forster Square Station behind the Midland Hotel.

(Left) Before Forster Square station was demolished the trackbed found a temporary new use in 1991, as a stable.

(Right) The long legs of a Pretty Polly model tower above the corner doorway of Sunwin House in a 1996 advertising promotion.

It's goodbye to the Victorian stonework of Forster Square Station as the demolition men do their worst in April 1992.

The finishing touches are put to the pavements around the refurbished Alhambra prior to its grand reopening as one of the jewels in Bradford's crown.

Snow on the ground during late-night shopping in Forster Square, photographed on 14 December 1983.

Provincial House remains under wraps on the right of this 1989 picture, taken from the police HQ, of the junction of Godwin Street and Thornton Road.

The end of the line wasn't yet in sight for the Odeon in March 1990, when this long queue formed for a special Saturday screening.

Chapter Seven

Looking to the Future

And so to the future. Imagine, if you will, Bradford city centre the year 2023. Water laps up to the edge of Centenary Square and a pier links the City Hall area to the National Museum of Photography, Film and Television.

Roaring traffic is replaced with a peaceful lake and a place to relax, gardens, lawns, apartments and quality shopping.

This is architect Will Alsop's vision of Bradford, part of the Masterplan that he was charged to create as a blueprint for ideal change in the city.

The masterplan was commissioned by the newly-formed Urban Regeneration Company and will be the basis for all the work carried out by the URC, now called Bradford Centre Regeneration, over the years ahead to draw millions of pounds of investment to the city, with spin-offs for the entire district.

The internationally-renowned architect and his team say they came to Bradford and found a great city with its landscapes obscured by buildings and its water courses diverted underground.

They came up with a radical vision of a city with a unique role and image, setting it apart from its neighbours instead of being compared unfavourably. The daring plan divides the city into four neighbourhoods – with City Hall at the heart of it. The Grade I listed building will stand in an oasis instead of what is virtually a traffic island.

Maud Marshall, chief executive of Bradford Centre Regeneration, described the master plan as a giant picture frame, which will be filled over the next two decades. Most of all, she hopes it will be inspirational and will get people talking in a city where many grandiose schemes have been proposed only to fail to get off the ground.

The master plan isn't set in stone. The proposed lake in the city centre might happen, or it might not. But it is a jumping-off point for a 20-year journey of regeneration. The message is, throw the rulebook out of the window. There are no rules. Bradford can be exactly what we want it to be. Ideas include demolishing the former Odeon Cinema and replacing it with an eye-catching sensory garden.

The next five to seven years will be used for the acquisition and demolition of properties, providing the platform for a rejuvenated city with landmark buildings and a booming economy.

Mrs Marshall said 'We are making a framework, which we hope will capture the imagination. But we are not going to produce things which are fashionable and here today and gone tomorrow. We need to bring a richness of development and designers. They must be iconic.'

Running parallel to the master plan, but an integral part of it because of its ethos of boldly redesigning Bradford city centre, is the Broadway scheme. Due to be finished in 2008, the £300 million project will sweep away the unattractive concrete edifices and replace them

Demolition begins on the Broadway redevelopment, with the destruction of office blocks.

with half a million square feet of bright new retail, office and leisure development. Work is already well underway and the old skyline of Bradford is being irrevocably altered to make way for what will be Bradford's true 21st-century landscape. Work has also taken place to transform the city's Kirkgate Market to create a more modern, pleasant shopping experience.

Under the auspices of the Connecting the City scheme, new roads are being laid out to make Bradford a much easier place to get around. With big name stores pledging to join the new development, as well as smaller, independent retailers to keep Bradford's identity, Broadway will soon be the focal point of the city centre. But that's not all: people are once more returning to live in the city centre, bringing the cycle of history covered by this volume almost full circle. Where once there were tenements and cramped housing, now there are airy, bright apartments for professionals, bringing Bradford alive with the atmosphere of general living.

It is truly a renaissance for Bradford, the creation of a city centre where its residents can live, work, shop and play, combining the best of the old with the excitement of the new.

Between the Broadway redevelopment and the various pieces of the Will Alsop master plan jigsaw, Bradford is facing change, the like of which it has never witnessed before. While this book is an historical record of Bradford's past, it is also a celebration of its future.

The massed ranks of demolition experts and equipment begin work on demolishing Broadway and redesigning Forster Square.

In the brave new world of Will Alsop's master plan, Centenary Square will be flooded and strange piers will jut out over the new city-centre lake.

A last look along Broadway before the demolition begins.

Leeds Road leading into Forster Square, with Hall Ings heading off to the left. A view that is changing forever.

A bird's-eye view of Broadway prior to the demolition work getting underway.

The BHS building at the bottom of Broadway.

Space-age designs for Bradford city centre from the mind of Will Alsop.

A futuristic Bradford… but could Alsop's dream for the city centre become reality?

The famous Will Alsop master plan for Bradford, with its infamous, comma-shaped lake skirting City Hall, its series of piers and the 'sensory garden' umbrellas to the left.

An aerial shot of Bradford city centre as it is now – compare and contrast this with Will Alsop's vision.

Part of the Alsop master plan is to ensure open space and interesting items across Bradford, such as this wetland area.

New frontage designs for Kirkgate Square, part of the Bradford city centre redevelopment.

Before the visions of the future become reality, much work needs to be done, as this shot of Forster Square shows.

Forster Square offices, about to be demolished.

The demolition squads move in to clear the way for a new Broadway.

Bring in the heavy guns… Forster Square offices are torn in two.

Clearing the way for the new Broadway redevelopment.

It might look a mess now, but you can't create a new Broadway without breaking a few old buildings…

The Cathedral in the background, to the right, looks over the massive pipes ready to be laid beneath the new road system.

The walls come tumbling down at Forster Square.

Valley Parade is in the distance to the right, while the Midland Hotel stands just behind the demolition work going on in the foreground.

The demolition brought with it new perspectives as Bradfordians saw the whole skyline changed.

The view across the demolition site with the Midland Hotel to the right and Cheapside straight ahead.

An aerial view of the new Bradford landscape emerging from the demolition work near Forster Square.

Office blocks are reduced to a tangle of metal and piles of rubble.

Forster Square office blocks are taken down piece by piece.

Looking from Forster Square at the area which will be totally redeveloped.

The Forster Square roundabout, centre-point of the new Broadway redevelopment.

The Forster statue in the foreground, with the old GPO building being demolished to the right.

More of Will Alsop's designs for Bradford, with the lake and City Hall near the top of the picture.

The new road system in place near Market Street, to allow demolition to continue apace.

Bradfordians at play in the futuristic surroundings of the sensory garden, part of the Alsop master plan.

Subscribers

Paul Richard Ackroyd
Rowland L Ackroyd
Mr & Mrs Leslie Ainsworth
Ernest Akers
Edmund Alderson
David M Allan
Nigel Allsopp
H W Ambler
Robert Ancliff
David Anderson
David Anderson
Colin Anness
Brian and Florence Appleyard
Colin L Appleyard
John David Artist
William Kitson Asquith
Keith Atkinson
Tessa Jean Atkinson
Allan Austin
Eric Austin
Mrs Lilian Aveyard
John Ayers
Eddie Aykroyd

Jack M Bailey
Richard Andrew Bailey
Kathleen & Brian Baines
Agnes Baker
Harry Baker
Jean Baker
Jenifer M Baker
Susan E Baker
Molly Balka
Susan Bannon
R D Banyard
Ray Banyard
Christine & Peter Baren
Peter B Baren
Ernest & Margaret Barker
Shirley M Barker
Steven Barker
Jacob Barnett
Gordon Barraclough
Pauline Barraclough
Philip Barraclough
Mary Barr
Robin Barratt
Tom Barrett
Keith Bartle
Alan Bedford
Doreen Mary Bedford
John Belcher
Arthur John Bell
Charles Bell
Jim & Essie Bell (Australia)
Ernest W Bennett
Marion Bennett

Susan Benson
Eric Bentham
Christine E Bentley Beaumont
Alan K Biggin
Jacqueline Billing
Josef Bodnarczuk
Joan Margaret Booth
Darren Borsos
John Malcolm Boswell
Marian Bottomley
David Bould
John Boyle
Bradford Centre Regeneration
J P Brady
Derek Brayshaw
Paul Kenneth Brayshaw
Horace Brewster
Paul Brian
Lawrence Leslie Brigg
Frank N Briggs
Mr Dennis Brimacombe
Reginald Brett Broadbent
Sue & David Broadbent
Howard Broadley
Gloria Evelyn Brogden
Valerie Victoria Brogden
Sydney Brooke
R Brookman
Mrs Alma Broome
Maureen Broscombe
Helen Brotherton
Gladys E Broughton
Margaret Rose Brown
Peter Brownbill
Mollie & Leo Brumfitt
Mrs Muriel Bryant
Brian Burke
David Burnet
Joyce Burns
Geoffrey C Burn
Nigel & Diane Burton
Ronald James Butcher
Matthew and Sue Butler
Harry Butterfield
Roger Butterfield
Joan Buzzard

Mrs Hilda Campbell
Allan Cansfield
Joseph Carolan
Barbara Carpenter
Sheila Carr
Michael David Carter
Richard S Carter
Mr Donald Cartwright
Stephen & Jennifer Cashman
David Paul Cathcart
Alice A Chapman

Barry Chapman
Harry Chapman
Rodney Chapman
John Charge
Linda Chiappetta
Colin Chippindale
Mike Chuck
Martin Clarke
Alan & Sandra Clayton
Peter Norman Clegg
H W Clough
Mary & Brian Connell
Peter Connolley
J Trevor Constantine
John, Linda, Anthony &
    Matthew Cook
Raymond W Cooper
Steven Cooper
Ian & Christine Copley
George C Cordingley
Philip Cordingley
N & J A G Core
Malcolm Couzens
Harry Cowan
Jean Craig
Ethel Craighan
Jane and David Craven
Roger & Judy Craven
Gillian Crisp (nee Cordingley)
Freda Critchley
Philip Crolla
Brian S Crossland
Matthew Crowther
Jack Cunningham

Mrs Betty Dalby
Dorreen Dale
Mr Jack Dale
B Danylczuk
Susan Darby
Chris Davey
Jackie Davies (nee Street)
Ernest Day
Arthur Deacon
Eric Dean
Winifred Dean
Christina Dennis
Ralph Denny
Christine & Allen Dickens
Alan Dickenson
Brian Dickinson
Frank & Jean Dickinson
Keith Dickinson
P J & L D Dickinson
John Dixon
Joyce & Tonie Dobby
Eric Dobson
Joan Dobson

John & Pat Dobson
J & R Dodd
Sheila Donaldson
Ian Dolby
Peter Dolby
Jack Doyle
Peter Drabble
Mrs Florence Dunn
Maureen Dunne
Mr Philip Dunne
John Drake
Peter Drake
David Drury
Doreen Drysdale
John Duff

P Eastaugh
David R Edmondson
Joyce Eggett
Doris Ellis
Harry Ellis
Ian Ellis
J Ellis
Ken Ellis
Ronald Ellis
Ronald Ellis (Australia)
Mrs Mavis Emmott
Barry Evans
Leslie Anthony Evans
Susan Evans
Tony Everson

Duncan and Sarah Farr
Brian E Farrelly
Mr & Mrs Keith Fearnley
Kath Feeley
Mark, Yvonne & Kimberley
    Feeley
Michael Feeley
David Fenton
Rosemary Fieldhouse
Dale Aston Finch
Doris M Firth (nee Dolly Taylor)
Doug Firth
Douglas Firth
George Firth
Graham & Angela Firth
Bernard Flanagan
Dennis Flatt
Marion Flaxman
Albert Foster
Mrs Pam Foster (nee Barron)
Margret Foster
Monica Mary Foulds
Paul Martin Foulds
Billy Frith
Bryan Furby